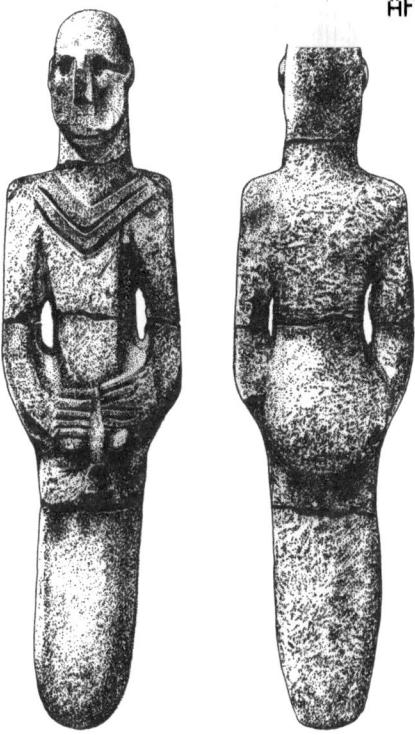

The Balikligöl Statue, or 'Urfa Man', was found in the oldest part of the city of Şanlıurfa at a site called Yenimahalle, dating from 8830 to 8650 BC. It has obsidian eyes, no mouth, a double v-neck garment, and a large stump at its base as though once planted in the ground.

First published 2023
This edition © Wooden Books Ltd 2025

Published by Wooden Books Ltd.
Glastonbury, Somerset.
www.woodenbooks.com

British Library Cataloguing in Publication Data
Newman, H.
Gobekli Tepe and Karahan Tepe

A CIP catalogue record for this book
may be obtained from the British Library.

ISBN-10: 1-907155-54-6
ISBN-13: 978-1-907155-54-3

All rights reserved.
For permission to reproduce any part of this
mega little book please contact the publishers.

Designed and typeset in Glastonbury, UK.
Printed in India on FSC® certified papers by
Quarterfold Printabilities Pvt. Ltd.

GÖBEKLI TEPE
AND KARAHAN TEPE
THE WORLD'S FIRST MEGALITHS

Hugh Newman

with original illustrations by Dan Lish and the author

I would like to dedicate this book to Klaus Schmidt [1953 - 2014] and would especially like to thank Andrew Collins, JJ Ainsworth, Stephen Parsons and John Martineau for their help and support in the production of this book, and to Dan Lish for the front cover and original artwork throughout the book. Thanks also to Ismail Can, Sabahattin Alkan, Ufuk and Neslihan Bölükbaşı, Howard Crowhurst, Graham Hancock, Adam Tetlow, Matt Sibson, Adora Gonzales, Rodney Hale, Matt Tweed and my family.

For further reading I would like to suggest 'Göbekli Tepe: Genesis of the Gods' by Andrew Collins (2014); 'Göbekli Tepe: A Stone Age Sanctuary in South-Eastern Anatolia' by Klaus Schmidt (2012); 'Prehistory Decoded' by Martin Sweatman (2019); 'Magicians of the Gods' by Graham Hancock (2015) and numerous articles and papers by Prof. Necmi Karul, Dr. Lee Clare and Bahattin Çelik.

ABOVE: *Enclosure D at Göbekli Tepe.*   TITLE PAGE: *Enclosure D and C at Göbekli Tepe.*

Introduction	1
The Neolithic Revolution	2
Before Göbekli Tepe	4
Göbekli Tepe	6
The First Stone Circles	8
The T-Shaped Pillars	10
Stone Reliefs	12
Ancient Animals	14
Pillar 43	16
Ancient Astronomy	18
Archaeoacoustics	20
Geometry & Measure	22
Cup Marks & Holes	24
Building Göbekli Tepe	26
Karahan Tepe	28
The Site	30
The Pillars Shrine	32
Solstice Alignments	34
Master Masons	36
Karahan Tepe's Structure	38
Keçili & Harbetsuvan	40
Sefer Tepe	42
Çayönü, Kilisik & Gürcütepe	44
Nevalı Çori	46
Sayburç & Ayanlar Höyük	48
Neolithic Religion	50
Language & Symbols	52
Who Were the Builders?	54
Ancient Geodesy	56
The Expansion	58

ABOVE: Central Pillar, Enclosure C. After a photograph by Oliver Dietrich.

INTRODUCTION

Göbekli Tepe ('potbelly' or 'navel' hill) is one of the largest megalithic sites in the world, and the oldest known example of monumental architecture. Located near modern-day Şanlıurfa (formally 'Urfa') in southeast Turkey, the earliest exposed structures currently date to 9,600 BC, a staggering 7000 years before Stonehenge.

The excavated enclosures at Göbekli Tepe contain scores of intricately carved T-shaped pillars, laid out in circular or oval configurations. There is evidence for astronomical alignments informing certain features of the design. Göbekli Tepe sits within a wider area known as 'Taş Tepeler' (stone hills). At least eleven more sites are located within this 124 mile (200 km) wide upland zone, including the prominent site at nearby Karahan Tepe.

Who built these incredible structures? Why and how did they do it? They appear just before the Neolithic transition to agriculture, prompting comparisons with the 'Garden of Eden'. Was this culture the first intersection between the old world of hunter-gatherers and the new world of settlers and farmers?

So extraordinary are these sites, and so early, that some people have suggested the builders of Göbekli Tepe and Karahan Tepe were the Watchers of the Old Testament, the Anunnaki deities of Sumerian tradition, or even remnants of an Atlantean civilisation who survived the ravages of the last Ice Age. Whoever they were, they seem out of place and out of time, as such sophistication was previously only thought to emerge in Sumer and Egypt some 6000 years later. Göbekli Tepe has rewritten the history books.

THE NEOLITHIC REVOLUTION
the dawn of civilisation

In around 10,800 BC, the Younger Dryas event triggered a global environmental cataclysm, ushering in a mini Ice Age in the Northern Hemisphere which lasted around 1200 years. Archaeologists define the early Neolithic era which follows this catastrophe as the Pre-Pottery Neolithic (PPN). This is subdivided into PPNA (c.10,000–8800 BC) and the PPNB (c.8800–6500 BC).

The PPN witnesses the beginning of the Neolithic Revolution—the transition from hunter-gathering to agriculture. This process spans thousands of years, varying in pace across different regions. Levantine sites within the Fertile Crescent, such as Jericho in Israel, have long been considered the most likely origin sites for this shift.

However, a smaller area within the crescent, the Golden Triangle, encompassing the Taş Tepeler sites, is posited as the location for a pivotal event in this story: the adaptation of einkorn and emmer wheat from wild grass to domesticated crop. Some archeologists now describe the Triangle d'Or as the 'cradle of agriculture', a place where, for better or worse, a new way of life was made possible. Quite how Göbekli Tepe meshes with this shift is still subject to investigation.

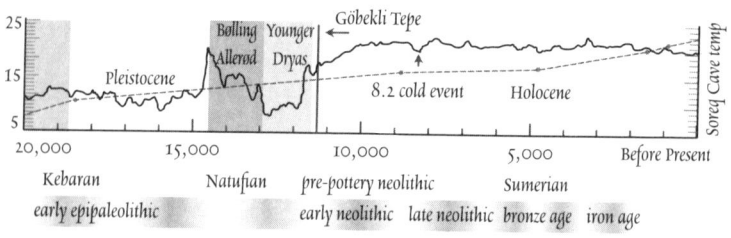

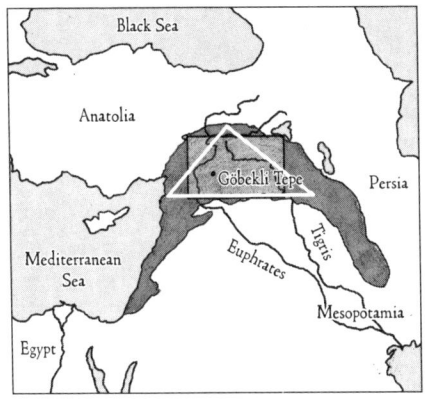

LEFT: The Fertile Crescent and The Triangle d'Or. The Fertile Crescent spans an area including southeast Turkey, Iraq, Syria, Lebanon, Palestine, Israel, Jordan, and Egypt. The Golden Triangle is centred around Karacadağ Mountain, between the northern ends of the Tigris and Euphrates rivers. Wheat, barley and the other Neolithic founder crops are concentrated here. New finds are constantly updating our understanding of this region and its role in the transition from hunter-gathering to a settled agricultural lifestyle.

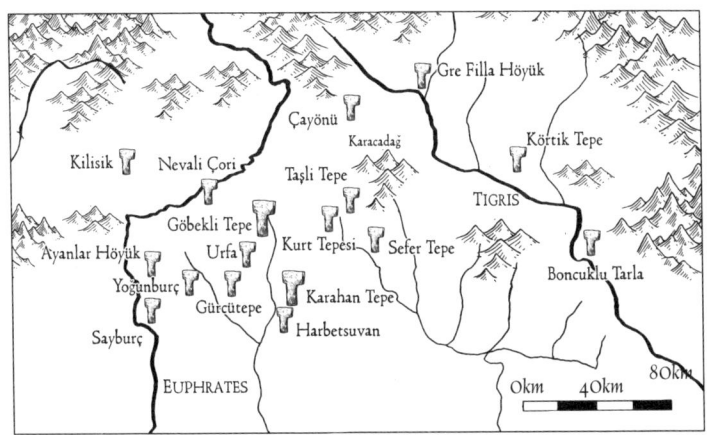

ABOVE: Map showing the Taş Tepeler sites featured in this book.
FACING PAGE: Changes in temperatures in the Post-Glacial period. The Pre-Pottery Neolithic (PPN) roughly corresponds to the period of warming in the Holocene.

BEFORE GÖBEKLI TEPE
the Tigris River settlements

On the upper reaches of the Tigris River are several archaeological sites that predate Göbekli Tepe. Roughly 62 miles (100km) east of Göbekli Tepe, the small settlement at Körtik Tepe dates to the Younger Dryas (10,800 BC). Unearthed from beneath a mound are the remains of well constructed stone houses and beautifully decorated artefacts, similar to those found at later sites across Taş Tepeler. There is also evidence of ritualistic burials, with plaster and paint applied to human remains.

At nearby Boncuklu Tarla (beaded field), excavations have revealed 30 dwellings, 6 public structures and the skeletons of 130 individuals. Raw copper items and more than 100,000 ornamental beads have been unearthed, with similar examples found at nearby Gre Filla Höyük. The square temple area is 9.2m (30ft) wide, and contained in one of its walls is a holed stone (*see examples on page 24*), which may have been used for very early astronomical observations.

Later in their timeline, these hunter-gatherer societies may have traded with those in Taş Tepeler, exporting knowledge and artistic practices. Alternatively the builders of Göbekli Tepe may originate from this Eastern region. Other important sites from this period include Gusir Höyük, Hasankeyf and Gre Fılla Höyük.

ABOVE: The square enclosure at Boncuklu Tarla. Finds date from the Epipaleolithic to late PPNB.
FACING PAGE: Körtik Tepe artefacts with carvings of abstract figures, serpents and chevrons.

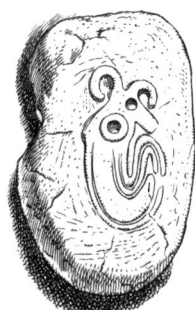

ABOVE: Relief carving on a small stone uncovered at Körtik Tepe in a similar style to that of Göbekli Tepe.

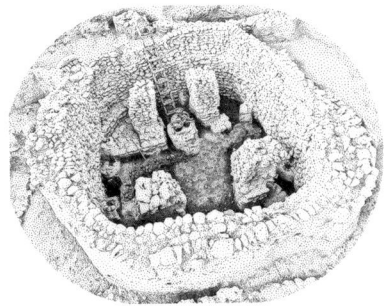

ABOVE. One of three examples of semi-subterranean buildings at Gre Filla Höyük; four large pillars constructed from smaller stones supported a roof.

GÖBEKLI TEPE
the sacred mound & the wishing tree

On the highest point of a limestone plateau, 7 miles (12km) northeast of Şanlıurfa in the Germuş Mountains, sits a solitary mulberry tree known in legend as the 'wish tree'. In 1963 archaeologist Peter Benedict arrived here and surveyed the area. He and his team noticed mounds of reddish soil separated by depressions, Neolithic flints, and Islamic 'tombstones'.

Little more was heard until 1994 when German archaeologist Klaus Schmidt investigated the site and realised the gravestones were in fact the tops of T-shaped pillars (*see below*), similar to those he had discovered a few years earlier at Nevalı Çori, dating to 8500BC (*see page 46*). Schmidt led excavations from 1996 until his death in 2014.

The discovery sent shockwaves across the archaeological world; here was evidence that hunter-gatherers built monumental architecture *before* the widespread transition to a settled agricultural lifestyle.

Schmidt said the hill (entirely man-made) was reminiscent of a pregnant woman's belly, the 'mound of first creation'. He and fellow archaeologists described it as a 'hill sanctuary', built for feasting, worship, and ritual.

Other archaeologists interpret the site slightly differently. Thomas Zimmermann suggests it was both settlement and ritual space; the 'last stand' of a society pushing back against the transition to agriculture, edifying their way of life.

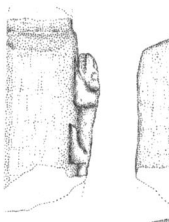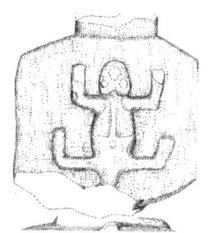

ABOVE: Göbekli Tepe before excavation. Göbek in Turkish can translate as 'heart, core, navel or centre.' In Kurdish the site is known as Girê Navoke, meaning 'navel-like hill', and Girê Mirazan, 'hill of wishes'. In Armenian it is known as 'Portasar'. It gained World Heritage status in 2018.

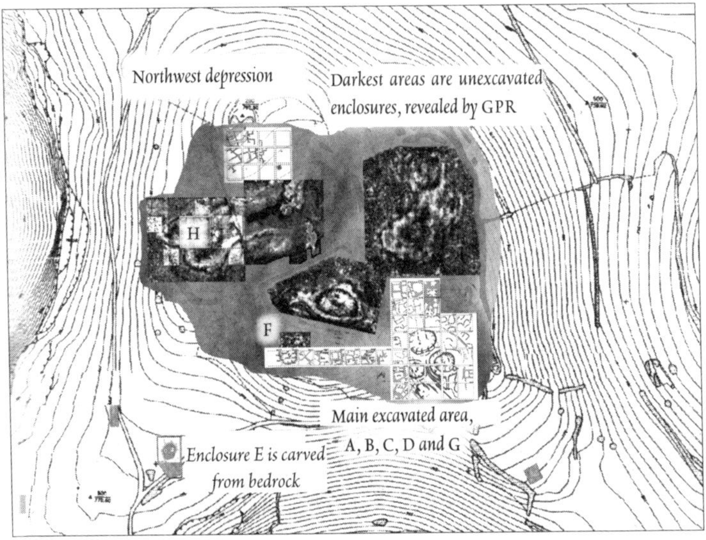

ABOVE: Topographical map of Göbekli Tepe with ground penetrating radar survey. The site covers an area of 9 hectares (22 acres). The white-squared sections are under excavation.

THE FIRST STONE CIRCLES
mysteries of the enclosures

The most prominent features of the archaeological site at Göbekli Tepe are its circular limestone enclosures. These monumental structures are part of its early construction phase, known as 'layer III' (dating to the PPNA, 9600 BC). All contain two central anthropomorphic T-pillars with smaller monoliths embedded in surrounding drystone walls. So far, five enclosures have been excavated with at least 20 more still guarding their secrets below ground.

Enclosure C is the largest at 22m (73ft) wide with two concentric circles. Enclosure D has 12 T-pillars in its perimeter, one being the magnificent Pillar 43 (*see p.16*), plus a porthole stone in the north (*see p.24*). In the centre are the two largest T-pillars at the site (*see p.11*).

Rectangular enclosures, part of a later phase of construction ('layer II', early and middle PPNB, 8800 BC onwards) have been found in the northwest depression. Some contain fire hearths, flints and bone tools; indicating domestic or artisanal use. Similar two-level 'houses' are found near the main enclosures; some have a T-pillar between a bench that may have supported a roof. Visiting pilgrims may have used these auxiliary spaces for accommodation and ritual activity.

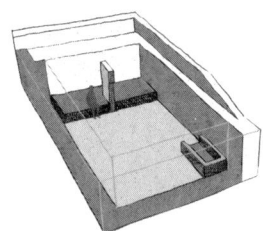

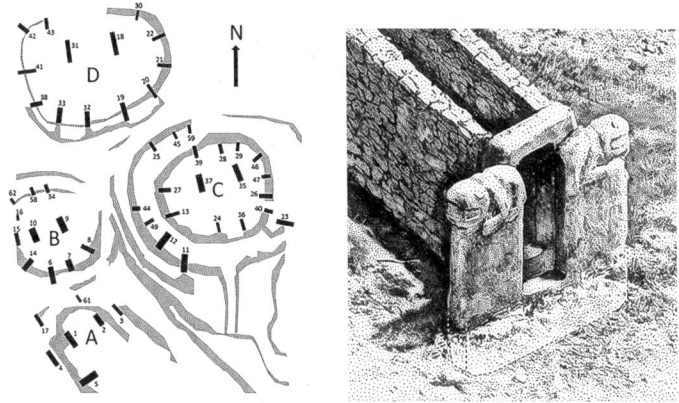

ABOVE LEFT: Four of the excavated enclosures at Göbekli Tepe, (after Rodney Hale et al). Enclosure A is only partially excavated, one of its T-pillars appears to be the wrong way round. It is slightly rectangular and could indicate the transition to the later phase (layer II). ABOVE RIGHT: Stone 'dromos', or ceremonial walkway, Enclosure C. (It reminded K. Schmidt of Tholos tombs in Greece).

ABOVE: Artist impression of Enclosure C and D under construction (after Fernando Baptista). Walls define the boundaries of each circular space, and provide structural support for the surrounding pillars; raised bedrock sockets may have held outer T-shaped pillars in place before outer walls were constructed.

The T-Shaped Pillars
humans, belts & 'H's

Göbekli Tepe's enigmatic T-shaped central pillars stand alone in the centre of their enclosures, most 'gaze out' towards the south. With carved arms down the widest side, hands touching the navel on a thin 'front', and a rectangular head (but no face), they appear to depict stylised humans. Sitting in shallow bases carved out of the bedrock, it is not clear how they remained upright (*see page 26*). The tops are often covered in cup-marks, coved out of the stone (*see page 24*).

The smaller T-pillars, built within the outer walls, surround these central figures like disciples looking at their masters. They are less humanlike, but feature carved reliefs of animals, symbols and other scenes. Miniature T-pillars have also been found, perhaps serving as amulets for pilgrims. Most of the sites we examine in this book follow this unique style for nearly 2000 years.

T-shaped pillars appear in other parts of the world. In Menorca, for instance, the Bronze Age Taula sanctuaries have similar enclosures but only one gigantic central T-pillar.

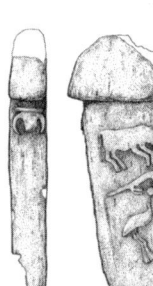
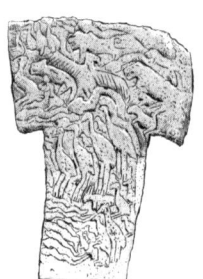

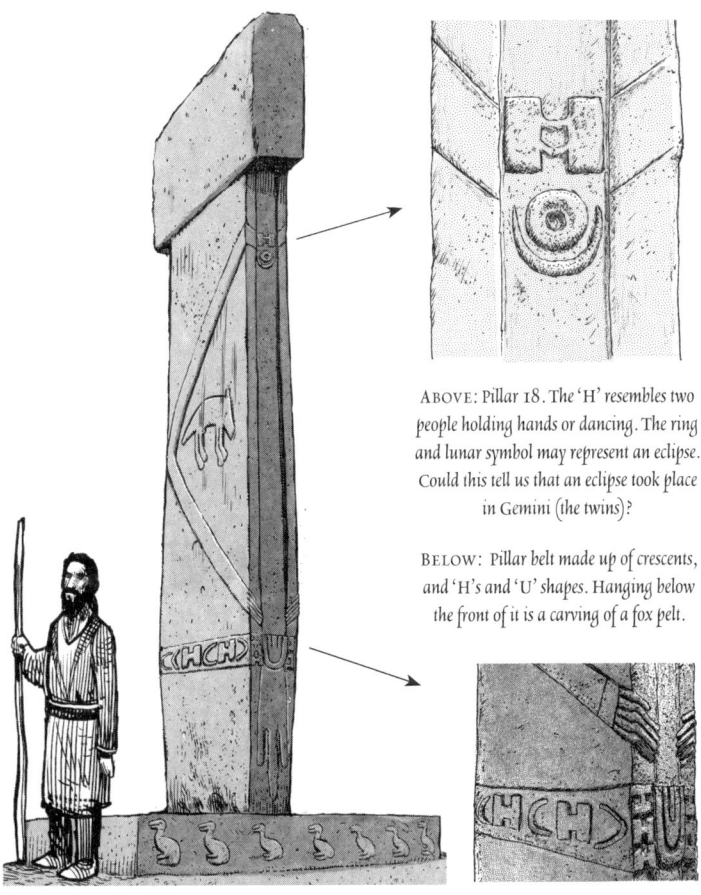

ABOVE: Pillar 18. The 'H' resembles two people holding hands or dancing. The ring and lunar symbol may represent an eclipse. Could this tell us that an eclipse took place in Gemini (the twins)?

BELOW: Pillar belt made up of crescents, and 'H's and 'U' shapes. Hanging below the front of it is a carving of a fox pelt.

ABOVE: The 5.5m (18ft)-tall Pillar 18 in Enclosure D. Seven flightless birds are carved into its base. Do these abstract forms honour ancestors, gods or a priestly elite? Are they wearing hoods? FACING PAGE, LEFT TO RIGHT: Lion / leopard on monolith in 'Lion Pillar Building'; Auroch, fox and crane on a central pillar in Enclosure A with relief on thin edge; 56 animals on Pillar 55, Enclosure H.

STONE RELIEFS
secrets of the master masons

The stone relief carvings of Göbekli Tepe show remarkable levels of craftsmanship and artistic expression. This is all the more impressive given that their creation predates the use of metal tools. Working in-situ, this highly intricate work was undertaken by a skilled team of stonemasons using tools made from materials such as antlers, flint and obsidian. A single mistake could ruin an entire monolith.

Low-relief carvings are the most numerous across the site but there are some stunning examples of high-relief figures (*see opposite*).

Animal motifs feature prominently but there are also geometric patterns such as chevrons, anthropomorphic figures, phalluses and other symbols. One of the rare female figures is etched into the stone (*see page 50*). Carved stone bowls and plates have also been found.

There appears to be little change in style over the 2000-year period the site was in operation. The purpose and meaning of these carvings are still subject to interpretation, but they provide tantalising clues into the cultural and ritual practices of this ancient society. Three-dimensional carving goes back nearly 40,000 years in Europe (*below*).

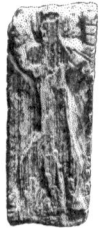  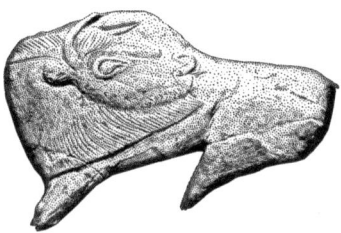

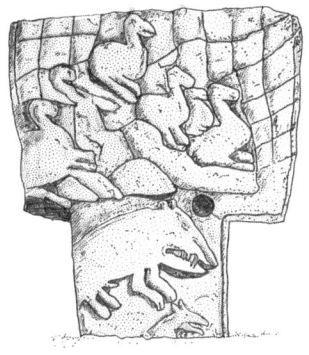 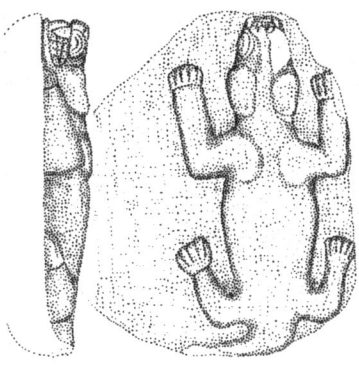

ABOVE: LEFT: Pillar 12 in Enclosure C. RIGHT: A lizard in high relief (after Klaus Schmidt).
FACING PAGE L-R: Carved mammoth ivory, Geißenklösterle cave near Blaubeuren, Germany, c.38,000 BC; The Venus of Laussel, Dordogne, France; Carved antler (c.15,000 BC).

 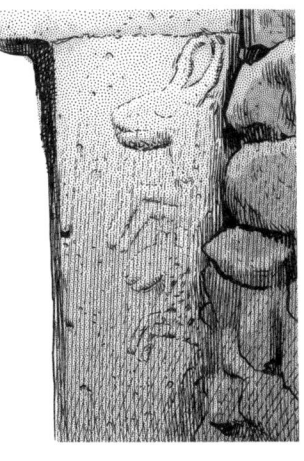

ABOVE: Pillar 27 in Enclosure C showing high relief of a snarling predator.

ABOVE: Pillar 21, Enclosure D, low relief of goitred gazelle and Asiatic wild ass.

Ancient Animals
noah's ark in stone

Animal carvings dominate the iconography at Göbekli Tepe. In Enclosure A the snake prevails, in Enclosure B foxes, in C boars, and in D birds take centre stage.

Across the site generally (and at other Taş Tepeler locations such as Karahan Tepe) serpent symbolism is the most prevalent. On some pillars multiple carved snakes overlap, in others they are parallel to one another in relief. Some face upwards, some downwards, some sideways. The serpent symbol is found in ancient cultures the world over, often associated with rebirth, renewal, and the underworld.

The fox is also a prominent symbol at the site. This is followed by bulls, aurochs, scorpions, cranes, canids, leopards, auks, ducks and creatures yet to be recognised. Some animals are carved grinning or ferociously baring their teeth. A life-sized wild boar statue with red, black and white pigments was unearthed in Enclosure D below the porthole stone *(see below)*. These may be 'guardians of the enclosures'.

While exact meanings are lost to us, this menagerie in stone would have made sense to its builders, depicting complex mythological, cosmological or hunting narratives *(see page 16)*.

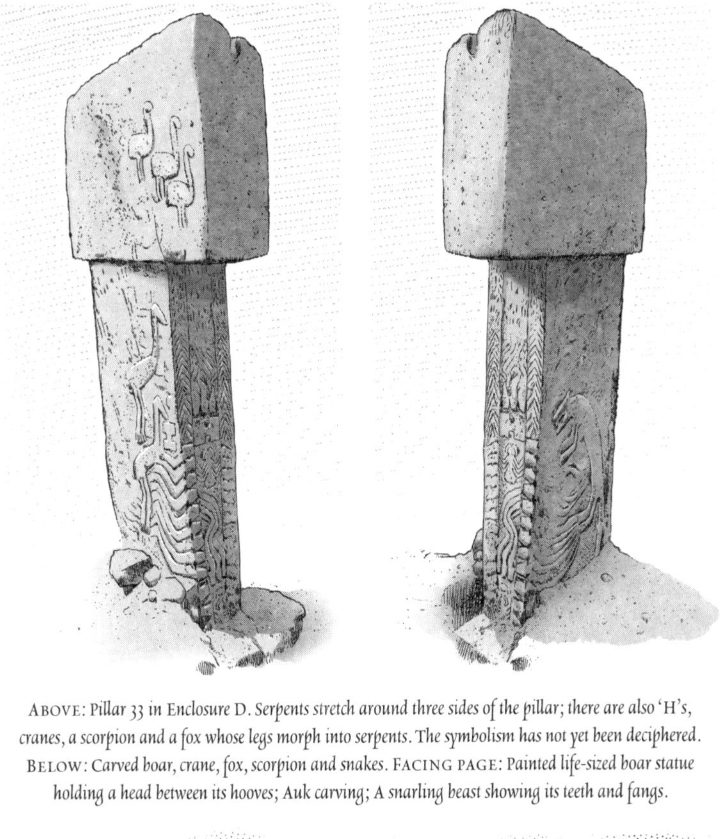

ABOVE: Pillar 33 in Enclosure D. Serpents stretch around three sides of the pillar; there are also 'H's, cranes, a scorpion and a fox whose legs morph into serpents. The symbolism has not yet been deciphered.
BELOW: Carved boar, crane, fox, scorpion and snakes. FACING PAGE: Painted life-sized boar statue holding a head between its hooves; Auk carving; A snarling beast showing its teeth and fangs.

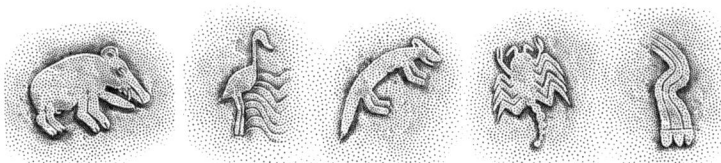

Pillar 43
the vulture stone

Pillar 43, or the Vulture Stone, in the northwest outer wall of Enclosure D is the 'Rosetta Stone' of Göbekli Tepe. It may be the world's first pictograph. Interpretations of its enigmatic motifs and narrative symbolism are many and varied. The three elements at the top could be sunrises, bags to carry sacraments, or the enclosures themselves—they look very similar to the skull building at Çayönü (*see page 33*). Italian archaeoastronomer Giulio Magli suggests they may be forerunners to the Babylonian 'houses in the sky', representing Enlil and Enki; the central T-pillars in Enclosure D may also depict these or other deities.

Dr. Martin Sweatman views Pillar 43 as map of the sky circling the Sun (the central ball) on the winter solstice in 10,950 BC, marking the Younger Dryas event (*see page 2*).

Author Andrew Collins suggests the ball is the northern celestial pole in 9600 BC (the year of construction); in his view the vulture marks the pathway of the soul after death in the area of Cygnus, the Dark Rift in the Milky Way. He also speculates that the ball could be a human head detached from its body.

JJ Ainsworth says that it represents the cycle of life, death and rebirth with the soul carried by a 'vulture shaman' through the 'Golden Gate of the Ecliptic'. In ancient Egyptian and Mesopotamian traditions the vulture is a 'psychopomp', a being that guards the entrance to the otherworld and carry souls to the afterlife. The scorpion on the lower panel may represent the constellation of Scorpius (*see page 34*).

Whatever its deeper message, the Vulture Stone has sparked much debate; attempts to decode its secrets continue.

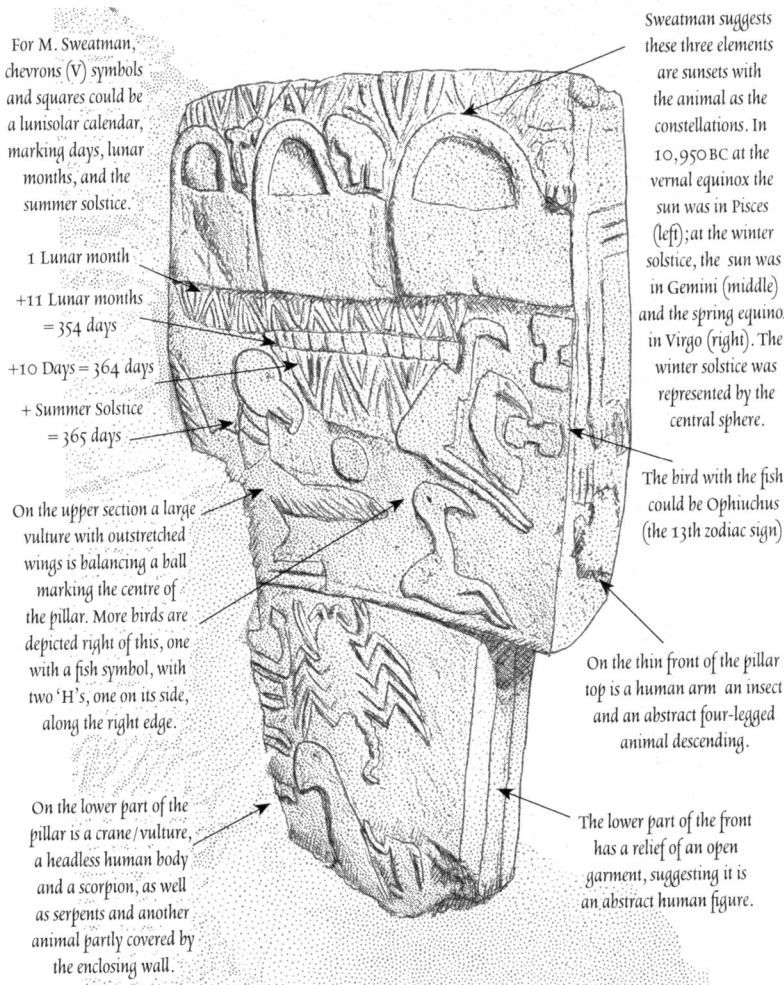

For M. Sweatman, chevrons (V) symbols and squares could be a lunisolar calendar, marking days, lunar months, and the summer solstice.

1 Lunar month
+11 Lunar months = 354 days
+10 Days = 364 days
+ Summer Solstice = 365 days

On the upper section a large vulture with outstretched wings is balancing a ball marking the centre of the pillar. More birds are depicted right of this, one with a fish symbol, with two 'H's, one on its side, along the right edge.

On the lower part of the pillar is a crane/vulture, a headless human body and a scorpion, as well as serpents and another animal partly covered by the enclosing wall.

Sweatman suggests these three elements are sunsets with the animal as the constellations. In 10,950 BC at the vernal equinox the sun was in Pisces (left); at the winter solstice, the sun was in Gemini (middle) and the spring equinox in Virgo (right). The winter solstice was represented by the central sphere.

The bird with the fish could be Ophiuchus (the 13th zodiac sign).

On the thin front of the pillar top is a human arm an insect and an abstract four-legged animal descending.

The lower part of the front has a relief of an open garment, suggesting it is an abstract human figure.

ANCIENT ASTRONOMY
the earliest star-gazers

Klaus Schmidt believed Göbekli Tepe was an open-air sanctuary, allowing the night sky to be observed from within. The intricate layout and orientation of the enclosures, aligned porthole stones, and carved symbols can all be linked with astronomical phenomena. Modifications over the centuries, with new pillars built over, or alongside existing ones, may have been attempts to re-orient enclosures to different parts of the sky. The Younger Dryas event had wreaked so much destruction, did Göbekli Tepe record this? Did it serve as an early warning system to spot comets? In some traditions fox tails are occasionally used to represent comets.

Later enclosures are oriented to the solstices. Enclosure F is orientated to the summer solstice sunrise. Karahan Tepe (9400 BC) is aligned to both solstices (*see page 35*).

Andrew Collins claims the mean azimuths of the central pillars of enclosures D, C, B, E and H all orient towards the gradual movement of the setting of Deneb, the brightest star of Cygnus in the north. Giulio Magli believes they were constructed to follow the rising of Sirius in the south, first being seen in the sky in 9300 BC. The three main enclosures appear to align in 9100 BC, 8750 BC and 8300 BC. However, Sirius may not have been visible at the time due to atmospheric extinction, the dimming effect on light of Earth's atmosphere.

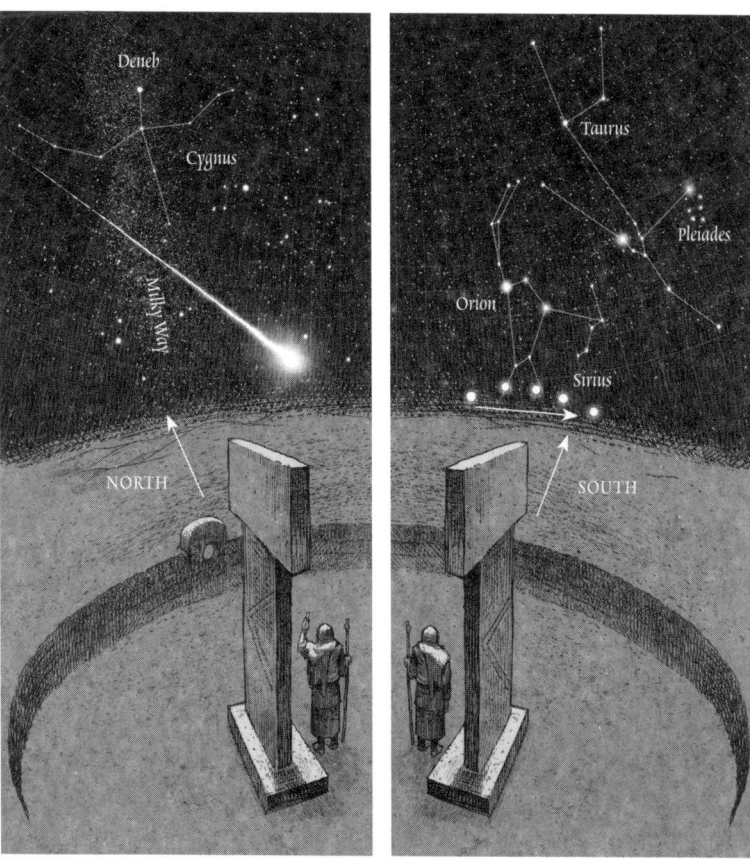

ABOVE: Imagined stargazing scene. LEFT: Northern orientation. The azimuths of central pillars in different enclosures track Deneb's setting position as it moves west over the centuries (Collins and Hale). RIGHT: To the south Sirius was visible above the horizon. At equinoxes, Orion, Taurus and the Pleiades appeared in the southern sky (R.Schoch). FACING PAGE: Carved bone, possibly showing Cygnus's 'belt stars' as three 'peck' marks above T-pillars.

ARCHAEOACOUSTICS
ellipses & altered states

Many of the enclosures at Göbekli Tepe are approximate ellipses. Andrew Collins noted that Enclosure D is a 4:3 ratio ellipse. A similar geometry is found in Enclosure C and H. Karahan Tepe and Jerf el Ahmar in Syria (c.9200 BC) have similar layouts. A 4:3 ratio relates to musical intervals, the perfect 4th. Collins also found these geometries and ratios in the grand design of the Giza pyramid complex. Acoustics engineer Steve Marshall noted them in West Kennet Long Barrow, near Avebury, in southwest England.

The placement of the seats in the outer walls is suggestive of a ceremonial or performance space. Low frequency instruments could have created infrasound, adding to the physiological and psychological effects on those gathered round.

Paolo Debertolis of University of Trieste carried out archaeoacoustic research at Göbekli Tepe and found similarities to other megalithic sites he had tested. Pillar 18 in Enclosure D, resonated around 68-69Hz with harmonics of 91Hz and 138 Hz. Its placement in a shallow pit enhanced the mechanism of vibration; was it designed to 'hum' in the wind like a tuning fork? A spiralling magnetic field was also recorded between the two central pillars.

More research and excavation will doubtless broaden our understanding, but there is much to suggest that the desire to harness natural energy flows or facilitate altered states played some part in the location, design and construction of Göbekli Tepe and other sites in the region.

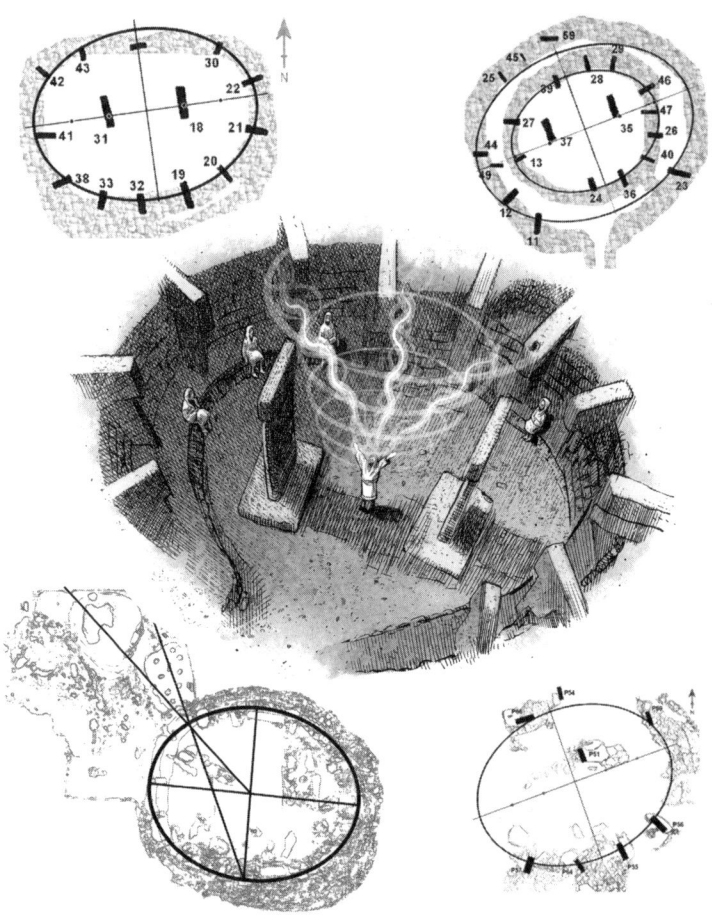

ABOVE: Elliptical-shaped enclosures at Taş Tepeler sites. UPPER: LEFT: Göbekli Tepe Enclosure D. RIGHT: Enclosure C. CENTRE: Artistic representation of acoustics being used in ceremonial activities. LOWER LEFT: Karahan Tepe ellipse orienting towards other features at the site. LOWER RIGHT: Enclosure H at Göbekli Tepe.

GEOMETRY & MEASURE
hidden triangles & ancient metrology

The design of Göbekli Tepe uses sophisticated geometry and ancient metrology, similar to the much younger stone circles in Britain and mainland Europe. Archaeologists Gil Haklay and Avi Gopher of Tel Aviv University have found an equilateral triangle that underlies the overall architectural plan of enclosures B, C and D (*see opposite*). The centres are located at the mean distance from the surrounding wall. A similar finding was made at Nevali Çori (*see page 46*).

The axis of symmetry on Enclosure D suggests it was built first with B and C planned around it. The entrances to these later enclosures are symmetrically positioned on both sides of the main axis, forming a neat arrow pointing towards the area of the sky containing Cygnus.

Using modular geometry to analyse the enclosures, Howard Crowhurst describes a triple-square system oriented perfectly NSEW. His analysis incorporates a diagonal angle between the central pillars of enclosures B and C, aligning with the main orientation discovered by Gopher and Haklay. The triangle was further analysed by geometer Adam Tetlow who found use of the Sumerian, Persian and Royal Egyptian feet, as well as the Sumerian Palm.

The geometric deductions of Alexander Thom can also be applied to these enclosures. Thom came up with eight variations on how British circles were laid out, three of these are found at Göbekli Tepe (*opposite*), and another at Karahan Tepe (*see page 30*).

All of this suggests that metrology and geometrical construction techniques are part of an extremely ancient knowledge system, reaching further into prehistory than was previously imagined.

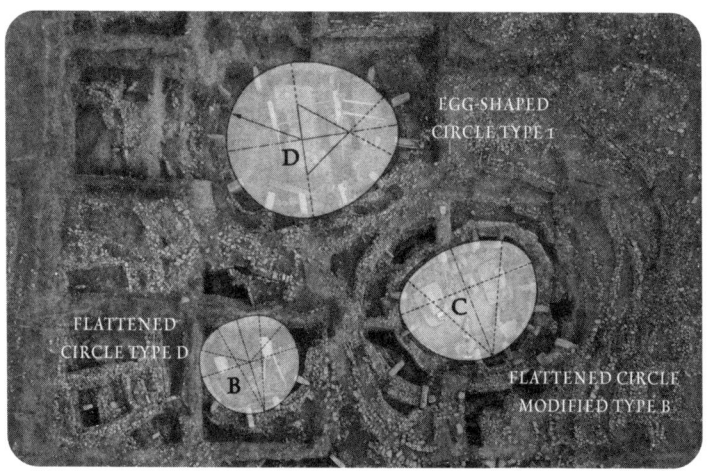

ABOVE: Hypothetical geometries of each enclosure based on the work of Alexander Thom.

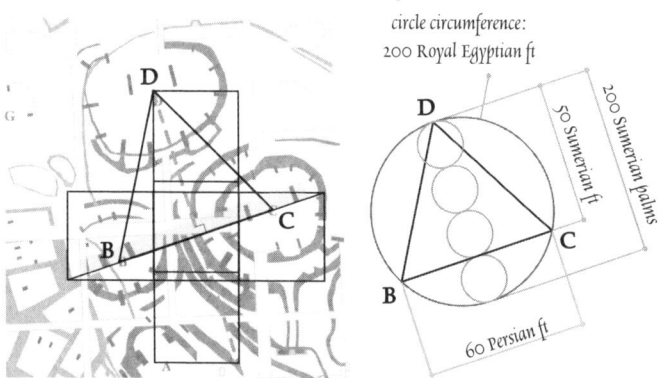

ABOVE LEFT: Geometric patterns at Göbekli Tepe (after Gopher and Haklay). Howard Crowhurst's analysis includes a cardinal alignment that is the traditional basis of temple construction.
ABOVE RIGHT: Adam Tetlow's plan of the hidden metrology found in Göbekli Tepe.

CUP-MARKS & HOLES
soul-holes & rock-carved bowls

Pre-Pottery Neolithic people carved out holes and cupules at many of their sites. Cup-marks, from a few inches to over 30cm (1ft) wide, were created by coving the stone with simple tools. They appear in exposed bedrock, floors, pedestals, and on the tops of certain T-pillars.

Theories explaining their use differ; they may have supported wooden posts, or served as spaces for plants, sacraments and oils. Those in elevated positions may have contained ritual offerings for carrion birds; the vulture is an important motif in Göbekli Tepe's carvings, crow and raven bones have been found across the site.

Rainwater that collected in these depressions may have been imbued with healing qualities; water on top of the T-pillars could have been reserved for a priestly elite. Interpretations abound.

Monumental porthole stones have been found on the floor and embedded in walls at Göbekli Tepe. Intricately carved, often placed in northern walls of enclosures, some align to Deneb (*see page 18*). Schmidt saw them as *seelenloch* (soul holes) through which spirits travel after death. Some examples have a beautiful 'frame' and relief carvings (*opposite*). More have been found at Ayanlar Höyük (*p.48*), Karahan Tepe (*p.28*) and Boncuklu Tarla (*p.4*).

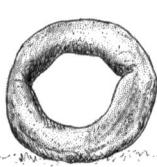

ABOVE: Cup-marks and two rectangular portholes in a stone, northwest depression, 3m × 3m (9.8ft). Overlooked by sculptures of a bull, ram, wildcat and 1.5 m (5ft) long snake. FACING PAGE, LEFT TO RIGHT: Holed-stone in Enclosure D with bird-like carving possibly signifying Cygnus; Circular stone ring, 60cm (2ft) wide; Holed stone, Enclosure B, flanked by two foxes and bull head; Cup-marks on T-pillar.

BUILDING GÖBEKLI TEPE
was it roofed & why did they bury it?

How was such a vast and impressive complex built? As far as we know, nothing like it anywhere on Earth had been attempted before. Scant evidence of construction techniques remain but Schmidt suggested that groups of hunter-gatherers collaborated in an organised, ritualistic manner, to quarry, carve, move and erect the stones.

Some of the oldest enclosures at Göbekli Tepe (also Çayönü and Nevalı Çori) have terrazzo floors. These are made of burnt lime and mortar which is left to cool and smoothed off, giving it a slightly mottled appearance; often they are colored red with ochre. Other floors are levelled out of the bedrock, from which shallow foundations were carved to hold up the pillars. Keeping the central monoliths permanently upright may have required beams, ropes or roofs (*see opposite*). How this tallies with theories which favour the 'open-air' enclosure model is uncertain. Supports could have been removed when the space was required for celestial observation or ritual.

In around 8000 BC the entire site was partially reconstructed and repaired, then, according to Schmidt, carefully buried under a vast mountain of stone, debris, and settlement refuse. Offering an alternative theory, Dr. Lee Clare suggests this 'fill' was from structures which slipped down the slope into the enclosures. Slippage may have occurred throughout its use, but recent evidence suggests it was completely buried once the decision was made to leave.

Did agriculture trigger the decline and closure of Göbekli Tepe, with human resources now required for labour intensive farming?

ABOVE LEFT: The quarry site, 500m from the enclosures. A 7m (22.9ft) unfinished T-pillar lies in-situ, it weighs 50 tonnes. Those standing in the enclosures weigh up to 16 tonnes. Smaller pillars, blocks, and rings also lie abandoned. Wooden rollers or a sledge may have been used to transport stones.

ABOVE RIGHT: Reconstruction of roof at Göbekli Tepe, (after E.Banning). A porthole stone, now on the floor, may have formed a roof entrance (as seen at Çatalhöyük). No wood has been found at the site.

ABOVE; Reconstruction of Göbekli Tepe (after Doğuş Group). On the right is Enclosure C. Enclosure D is behind, covered with animal skin and earth, and on the left is Enclosure B with a porthole entrance in a flat roof. In the background are rectangular buildings for domestic and ritual use, as well as for food / grain processing. Over 7000 grinding tools have been found across the site.

Karahan Tepe
Göbekli Tepe's sister site

Built into the side of a rocky hill in the Tektek Mountains, 23 miles (37 km) southeast of Göbekli Tepe, lies the enigmatic Karahan Tepe. This spectacular site dates from 9400 to 8200 BC (PPNA - PPNB) and covers 13 hectares (33 acres), an area larger than Göbekli Tepe. Its original name was Keçili Tepe (also the name of a hill to the north which has ruins). In Turkish, Keçili means 'bald'; in northern Kurdish (Kurmanji) it translates as 'woman, maiden, daughter or queen'.

Turkish archaeologist Bahattin Çelik noticed its importance in 1997 but until excavation began in 2019 only the tops of T-pillars and a few surface stones were visible. Prof. Necmi Karul of Istanbul University has since excavated the northern slopes revealing an astonishing 300 monoliths, mostly T-pillars, many of which depict humans, animals, and various symbols. There are large stone circle enclosures, rock-cut areas, unfinished monoliths, and an array of unique artefacts including spectacular statues and smaller carved objects (*see page 36*).

ABOVE: Excavated hill of Karahan Tepe. The 23m (75ft)-wide Structure AD, partly carved from the bedrock is the dominant feature (see page 31). At the time of writing, 5 percent of the site is excavated.
FACING PAGE: A 5.5m (18ft) unfinished T-pillar weighing 40 tonnes, western edge of Karahan Tepe.

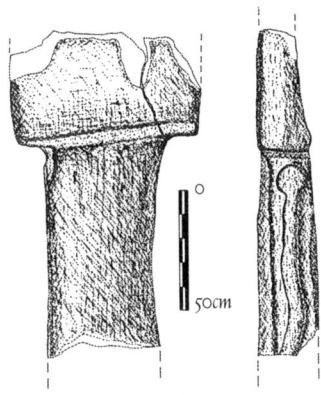

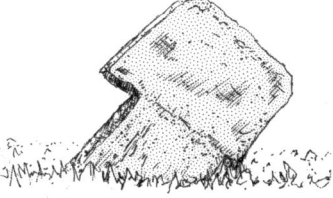

LEFT: The first discovery at Karahan Tepe was this T-pillar with a serpent carved in relief on its 'front' found by Prof. Bahattin Çelik. ABOVE: A T-pillar protruding from the ground before excavation.

The Site
megalithic thrones & hidden geometry

The main 'AD' structure at Karahan Tepe is 23m (75ft) wide (slightly larger than Enclosure C at Göbekli Tepe). There would have been 18 pillars around the edge with two larger monoliths (now broken and fallen) in the central area. The western side had five pillars carved out of bedrock, the others were free-standing in the perimeter. Between these bedrock pillars are stone thrones facing east. The bedrock was levelled to create the floor, with a terrazzo filling (*see page 26*).

Structure AD is an approximate ellipse shape with a ratio of 6:5 (or more accurately 32:27) suggesting potential acoustic properties (*see page 20*). Like Göbekli Tepe's enclosures, a more precise analysis of its geometry reveals it to be one of Alexander Thom's types, in this instance an 'egg-shaped circle with semi-elliptical end, type III'.

The massive central pillars in the enclosure may have been deliberately damaged before the site was covered over. Other T-pillars have carvings of leopards, serpents, canids and other animals. Some of the statues are now on display in Şanlıurfa Museum. The largest human statue at the site is 2.3m (7ft 6in) tall (*see page 36*).

Subsequent smaller enclosures were constructed at a later period. Large porthole stones have been found suggesting they were used as roof entrances. Some enclosures are tiny, with only one or two T-pillars, yet as building progressed, they spread out over a vast area across the hill.

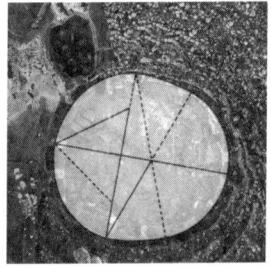

30

KARAHAN TEPE

N ↑

Structure AC
Partly built inside a bedrock outcrop; T-pillars were once inside it.

Structure AB
Also known as the Pillars Shrine.

Water may have played a major role at this site; carved channels link up certain enclosures, with deep holes cut into bedrock at specific locations.

'The Kitchen'
A kiln, stone plates and viper snake skeletons discovered.

Structure AA

FACING PAGE: Geometric plan of Structure AD. It is close to an Egg-shaped circle with semi-elliptical end, type III based on the surveys of Alexander Thom.

Structure AD

Structure AK

Structure AF

Structure 9K
Exposed in 2023 this enclosure is larger than Structure AD and is where the giant human statue, vulture and porthole stone were found (see p.37).

Structure AE

Structure AH
Square, with 4 standing T-pillars, a small porthole stone to the NE, and a V-neck statue with 8-fingers on each hand (see p.37).

THE PILLARS SHRINE
structure AB & the unfinished pit

Structure AB ('The Pillars Shrine') lies north of the main enclosure and measures 7m (21ft) by 6m (18ft). It has a trapezoidal plan with rounded corners containing 10 phallus-shaped pillars carved directly out of bedrock, and a thin, curved, free-standing monolith, inserted into a socket in the floor. These astonishing protrusions are overlooked by a carved head on the western wall. It has a pouting mouth which may represent 'talking'. It is three times the size of a human cranium, flattened on top, with serpent scales etched onto its neck.

On the southeast edge is a 70cm (2.2ft) wide hole leading out to the main enclosure. Steps on the south and northeast sides were used to descend into the area.

Standing 1.6 (4.5ft) to 1.7 (4.7ft) metres tall, the four pillars in front of the head are carved more elaborately than those in the back row which are 1 (3ft) to 1.4m (4ft) tall. Both structures were carefully filled in at the end of their use. Specific materials found in layers were entombed by larger slabs on top, forming a final stone roof.

The 'Unfinished Pit' (Structure AA) adjoins the Pillars Shrine. On its stone bench are impressive carvings of a serpent and fox.

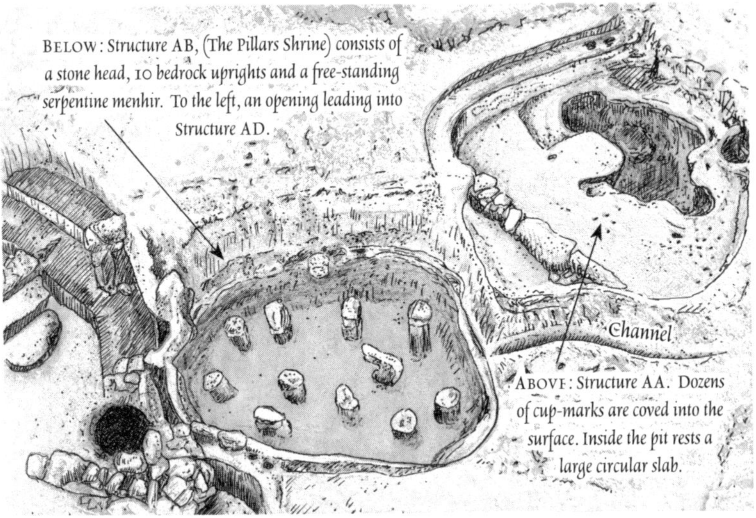

BELOW: Structure AB, (The Pillars Shrine) consists of a stone head, 10 bedrock uprights and a free-standing serpentine menhir. To the left, an opening leading into Structure AD.

ABOVE: Structure AA. Dozens of cup-marks are coved into the surface. Inside the pit rests a large circular slab.

ABOVE: Note the serpentine channel carved in the bedrock. This may have carried water into the Pillars Shrine, emptying through the porthole stone into a circular well in the main enclosure. Was this reservoir a phallic themed ceremonial area for male initiation rituals?

LEFT: Inside Structure AB looking towards the stone head with the free-standing pillar on the right.

FACING PAGE: Stone bench in Structure AA with serpent carving on the left. Fox torso and head on the right, two large cup-marks above it.

SOLSTICE ALIGNMENTS
the astronomy of Karahan Tepe

Karahan Tepe incorporates amazing solstice alignments. Ten minutes after sunrise on the winter solstice (Dec. 21st) the author and American researcher JJ Ainsworth observed a beam of light shining across the Pillars Shrine. Emanating from the porthole connecting to the main enclosure, this blade of light illuminates the protruding head for 45 minutes (*see page 32*). After a moment of darkness the sun rises higher in the sky and manifests a 'halo' of light around the top of the head. Taking the changing obliquity into consideration, in 9000 BC the head would have been illuminated more fully. Bright full moons at the summer solstice would have produced a similar effect.

The eyes of the head point towards the porthole stone, whilst the head faces east, towards sunrise at spring and autumn equinox. The constellation of Leo (perhaps seen as a leopard according to carvings at Karahan Tepe) appears at the same time. A channel is carved out of the bedrock from the Pillars Shrine running east.

Two more expansive sky and land alignments are shown opposite.

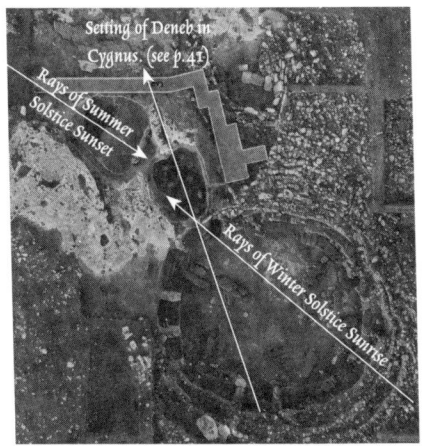 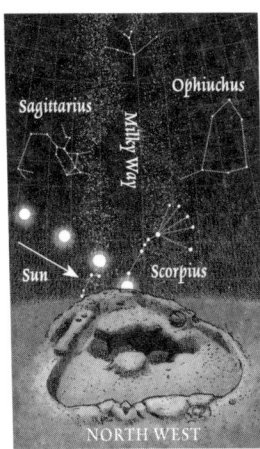

TOP LEFT: Three astronomical alignments at Karahan Tepe. TOP RIGHT: The Milky Way rose vertically 2½ hours after Midsummer sunset in 9000 BC, aligning along the orientation of the unfinished pit (after A. Collins).

ABOVE: Night and day at Winter Solstice in 9002 BC, 9010 BC, 9018 BC. The Milky Way rises horizontally at night, and Venus rises one hour before sunrise every 8 years. The winter solstice sunrise then occurs and shines through the porthole stone FACING PAGE: The stone head in the Pillars Shrine is illuminated by a blade of light moving left to right for 45 minutes during the winter solstice sunrise.

Master Masons
intricate artefacts & sublime statues

The excavation at Karahan Tepe has unearthed remarkable examples of 11,400 year old stonework and sculptures, including a 3.4m (11ft) tall anthropomorphic pillar with 8 fingers on each hand. As noted by Necmi Karul, not all the statues at the site have five fingers! In 2023 a 2.3m (7ft 6in) male statue and a 70cm (2ft 3in) tall vulture were found.

Ceremonial stone plates, up to 50cm (1.5ft) wide have been discovered on the stone benches between the T-pillars. The plates have small chips; were they used as stone drums? One has a cup-mark, suggesting sacramental use. Stone heads are embedded in walls throughout the site, some appear to be wearing masks. Other statues, some 'totem poles', or combinations of human and animal were found in the main enclosure, whilst others are broken or damaged. Small stone masks, beautifully carved basins and tiny totems of women, birds, frogs and other animals have also been discovered, as well as mysterious carved stone models with peculiar, almost surreal forms. Were these objects part of shamanic practice and ceremony?

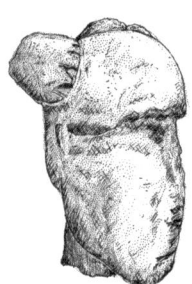  

BELOW: Some of the statues found at Karahan Tepe: a: Stone plate. b: T-pillar with 8 fingers (Structure AH). c: Stone frog. d: Canid mounting a human. e: Stone object with chevrons. f: Stone vulture. g: Humanoid statue with two foxes on front. h: Growling animal. i: 2.3m (7ft 6in) human statue.

FACING PAGE: LEFT: Masked head with two animal paws on its scalp. CENTRE: Frowning figure with elongated cranium, perhaps with mask and hood. RIGHT: A double-headed figure (aged human and young person) with animal paws on their heads.

KARAHAN TEPE'S STRUCTURE
did it have a roof?

The rock-carved uprights of Karahan Tepe's Pillars Shrine and the thrones on the western edge of Structure AD are unique in the Taş Tepeler region. Did the builders live here: eating, sleeping, hunting on the plains below, or was it a ritual space used at certain times of year for feasting, ceremony and performing?

The limestone geology of the Tektek mountains has no waterways. Rainwater for practical and ceremonial use was collected via stone-cut water channels and holes at specific locations (*see page 33*).

Roofs may have covered these enclosures, although no evidence of wood, required for construction, has yet been found. At the end of its use, Karahan Tepe was deliberately covered over and (like Göbekli Tepe) forgotten about until its discovery in 1997.

ABOVE: Reconstruction of Karahan Tepe with roof (after Bukafa Media). BELOW: The site during its heyday viewed from the south. FACING PAGE: Imagined celebration after winter solstice sunrise, with inset of leopard carving. Statues, stone plates and artefacts are shown where they were discovered.

KEÇILI & HARBETSUVAN
secrets in the Tektek Mountains

One mile (1.6km) to the north of Karahan Tepe lies another stony hill called Keçili Tepe. On the western side are two large man-made caves; on the southern slope the locally named 'snake pit' is one of several beehive hypogeums, covered by monumental holed stones.

On the northern summit is a curved stone outcrop and a square 'rock-temple' cut directly from the bedrock. It faces east with steps on one side (*see opposite*). Stone tools and flints have been found, thought to be contemporary with Karahan Tepe.

From the southern entrance of Structure AD at Karahan Tepe, through the porthole stone to the peak of Keçili Tepe (at a bearing of 340 degrees) the setting of Deneb in Cygnus lined up in 9000 BC, just as it does at Göbekli Tepe (*see page 19*).

Around 5 miles (7km) southwest of Karahan Tepe, Harbetsuvan Tepesi ('the ruined mound of flint') is a small-scale satellite settlement, measuring 95m (312ft) by 85m (279ft). In 2017, excavations found T-pillars and carvings in a style similar to Göbekli Tepe's later phases, being dated from 9000 to 8500 BC. There are carved fingers found on some pillars, and a section of a seated figure with phallus (*see opposite*).

Numerous square buildings 4m × 4m (13ft) have been found; they have no entrances so access was probably through the roof. A curved outer wall was also detected. In 2022, an early PPNA layer containing 2800 stone assemblages and beads gave an occupation date of 11,000 to 9500 BC, but no stone constructions were found at this level. There are also cavities carved out of bedrock, possibly to collect water.

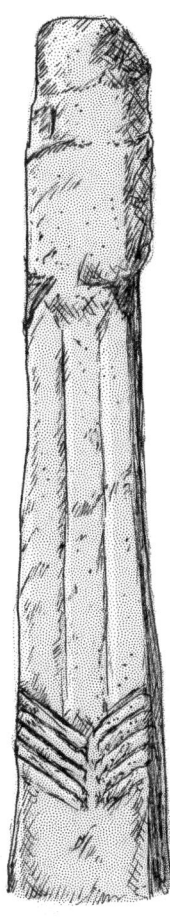

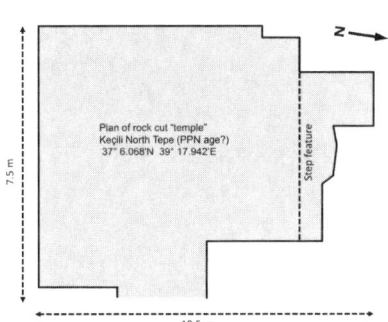

ABOVE: The 'Rock Temple' at Keçili Tepe is carved out of solid limestone. Plan by Andrew Collins and Rodney Hale. To the north is a small hypogeum, possibly dating to the time of Karahan Tepe.

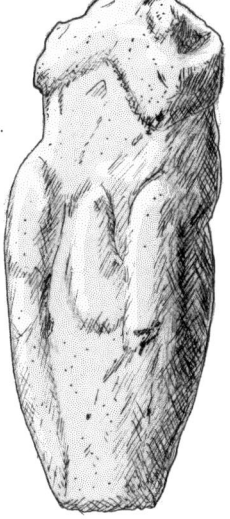

RIGHT: Figurine from Harbetsuvan Tepesi, seated male with phallus.

ABOVE: Broken stone T-pillar at Harbetsuvan Tepesi, with human hands and a V-neck, like that found on Urfa Man (see frontispiece) and the relief at Sayburç.

SEFER TEPE
& other Taş Tepeler sites

Sefer Tepe, 45 miles (72km) east of Şanlıurfa, is an important Taş Tepeler site (Sefer means "expedition" or "journey"). Dating to 8000 - 9000 BC, this low limestone mound covers an area of 1100 m² (11840 sq ft) and the quadrangular structures are built upon the bedrock. During initial excavations in 2003, 16 T-shaped pillars were found in-situ and a rare mortar found in the walls. A small limestone disc discovered in 2022 has 13 peck marks in different configurations on both sides, possibly representing a lunar calendar. Hundreds of beads have been found, one in the shape of a serpent's head. Bones of a 14-year-old and a 17-year-old human have also been unearthed. One T-shaped pillar is unique, boasting what looks like a bow-tie (*see opposite*)!

Kurt Tepesi (Wolf Hill) is a small settlement on a high limestone ridge overlooking the Coban Creek Pass. Part of the site has been illegally excavated and the tops of T-pillars still protrude just above the surface. T-shaped pillars up to 2.5m (8.2ft) tall have been found in the local village and flints discovered there date to 9000 BC, the same era as Karahan Tepe and layer II of Göbekli Tepe.

Northeast of Göbekli Tepe (where einkorn wheat was first domesticated), lies Taşlı Tepe, another Pre-Pottery Neolithic site. Small T-pillars, up to 1.5m (5ft) long, a terrazzo floor, a 30cm (1ft) wide stone plate (like those at Karahan Tepe) and a 2.5cm tall green stone bucranium pendant (*opposite*) have been uncovered. It is strategically located in relation to other Taş Tepeler sites and sits directly between the Tigris and Euphrates rivers on the slope of Karacadağ Mountain.

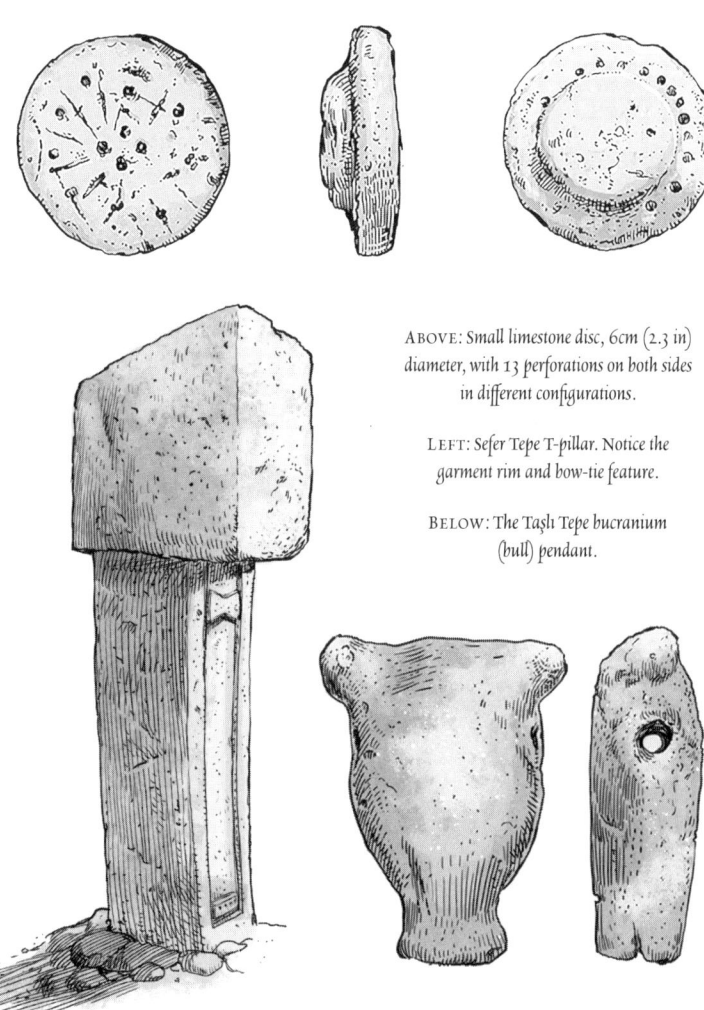

ABOVE: Small limestone disc, 6cm (2.3 in) diameter, with 13 perforations on both sides in different configurations.

LEFT: Sefer Tepe T-pillar. Notice the garment rim and bow-tie feature.

BELOW: The Taşlı Tepe bucranium (bull) pendant.

ÇAYÖNÜ, KILISIK & GÜRCÜTEPE
alien statues, goddess figurines & skull buildings

Northwest of Diyarbakır at the foot of the Taurus mountains, Çayönü Tepesi prospered from 8630 to 6800 BC (*see map, p.2*). Emmer wheat and some early evidence of pig domestication have been found at the remains of this settlement. Hundreds of human craniums were also uncovered, some of young people, indicating sacrificial rites may have taken place here. Standing stones in avenues were also found.

The strange Kilisik Statue was found near Adiyaman in 1965 (*see opposite*). Measuring 80 cm (32 in) in height, it is dated to 9000 BC. Perhaps inspiring the 'Alien' movie franchise, it appears to be wearing a hood; its hands hold up a garment revealing a hole on the front, suggesting it could be a female fertility idol.

Gürcütepe is located just southeast of Şanlıurfa in a built up area and consists of eight mounds. It was first excavated in 1995 by Klaus Schmidt (at the same time as Göbekli Tepe). One of the later PPNB sites of the region (8800 – 7000 BC), a 2021-22 dig uncovered more of the area revealing some large stone walls, pits, flint tools, stone axes and bone fragments. A limestone seated human amulet, a small carved animal and a rare goddess figurine were the highlights.

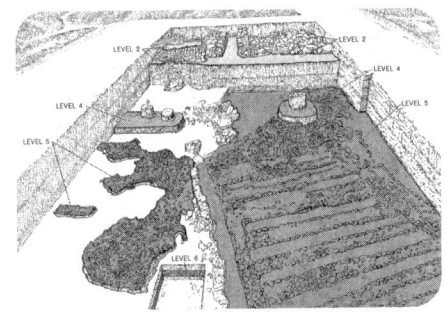

ABOVE LEFT: Double-headed female figurine from Çatalhöyük. RIGHT: Various levels at Çayönü, (after H. Çambel and R. Braidwood).

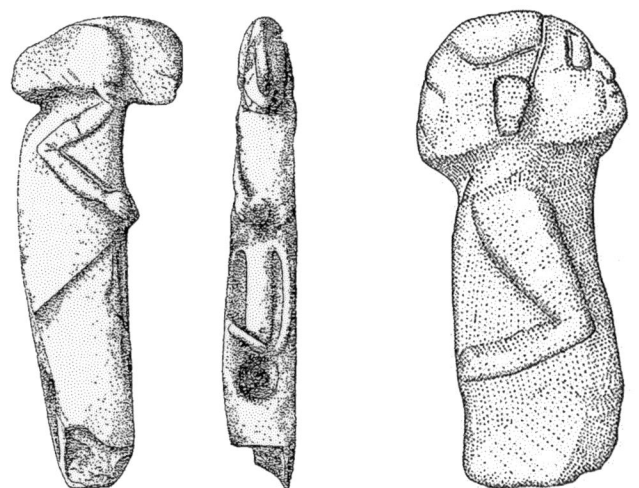

ABOVE LEFT: The 80 cm (32 in) high Kilisik Statue, (after, M. Verhoeven). ABOVE RIGHT: A similar statue found in the same area (Gazientep Museum, after K. Schmidt). The arms are similar to those carved on larger T-pillars. FACING PAGE. LEFT: Goddess figurine from Gürcütepe, resembling those found at Çatalhöyük and Malta. RIGHT: Two buildings at Çayönü Tepesi with terrazzo floors.

NEVALI ÇORI
settlement of the serpent people

Located on both banks of the Kantara stream, a tributary of the Euphrates (*see map page 3*), Nevalı Çori or 'Valley of the Plague' was a huge settlement, its excavated buildings contemporary with the later phases of Göbekli Tepe (8400 BC onwards). Klaus Schmidt was involved in the initial excavations, led by Harold Hauptmann between 1983–1991. Just before the area was to be flooded to serve the Atatürk Dam, the site was dismantled stone-by-stone, and much of it moved to the Şanlıurfa Museum.

Alongside carved statues, stone 'totem poles' and large dwellings was a unique cult structure called the 'Terrazzo Building'. Its corners were aligned cardinally, leaving the temple facing almost exactly SW.

Twenty-three domestic structures, one measuring 16m (52ft) by 7m (23ft), included animal fat lamps for illumination, as well as underfloor channels allowing cold water to flow in from the stream, possibly an early attempt at air conditioning. A stone head found at the site with a serpent on the back looks very much like a *shikha*, a tuft of hair worn by Vedic priests from the Indian subcontinent.

Evidence of very early cultivation and domestication of einkorn wheat were also found, predating the material remains.

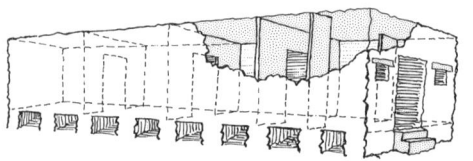

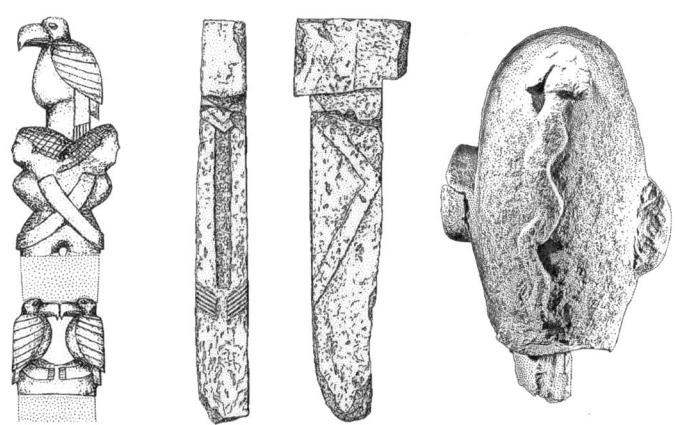

ABOVE LEFT: Totem pole. MIDDLE: Interior monoliths with V-neck designs and hands touching the navel (after H. Hauptmann). ABOVE RIGHT: Stone head found in the square temple. FACING PAGE. LEFT: The world's first air conditioned home? RIGHT: Twins dancing with a turtle on a stone vessel.

ABOVE: Artist drawing of the 'cult structure'. Workers lay the 80 m² (860 sq ft) terrazzo floor. It is 15 cm (5.9 in) thick, and contains about 10–15% lime. INSET LEFT: Avian statue 60cm (2ft) wide. RIGHT: The 'Bird Man' statue could be a representation of biblical 'Angels' or 'Watchers' wearing a hood wrapped in what appears to be wings.

Sayburç & Ayanlar Höyük
& other nearby sites

The village of Sayburç (*say* = counting, *burç* = zodiac sign/horoscope), is located upon a raised mound 12.5 miles (20 km) from Şanlıurfa. In 2021 it was the scene of a stunning discovery: a five-figure carved stone panel was unearthed from under a house, part of a PPN enclosure.

The 11,000-year-old carving details two leopards, a bull, a jumping man with 6 or 7 fingers on one hand holding a serpent (or bola), and a 3D high-relief carving of a man with a V-neck and phallus.

Nearby Ayanlar Höyük is the third largest site identified with only a small section investigated. Its Kurdish name is Gre Hut—'giant that eats'. Stunning artefacts have already been unearthed there (*see opposite*). Yoğunburç and Çakmaktepe are nearby Taş Tepeler sites.

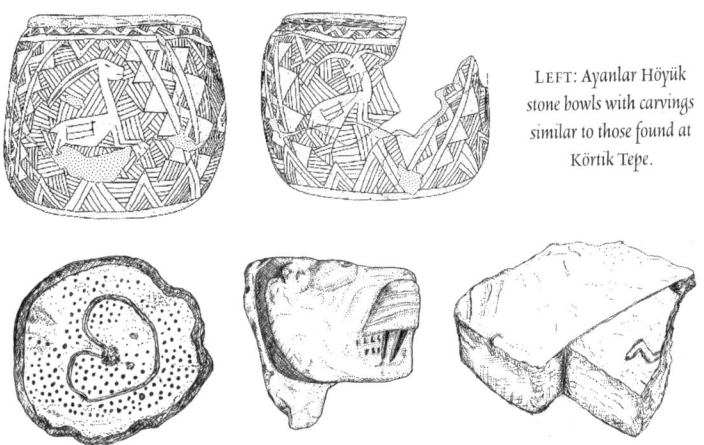

LEFT: Ayanlar Höyük stone bowls with carvings similar to those found at Körtik Tepe.

ABOVE LEFT: A 14 inch wide carving found on bedrock near the Sayburç panel, with a snake-head centre
CENTRE & RIGHT: Leopard relief and T-shaped pillar fragment from Ayanlar Höyük.

NEOLITHIC RELIGION
shamanism, skull cults & the goddess

There is plenty of evidence for ritual activity at Göbekli Tepe and surrounding sites, but did the builders of these extraordinary structures have an organised religion? What kind of spiritual practices did they have? Did they worship gods and goddesses?

Modified skulls have been found at Göbekli Tepe suggesting a cultic process, previously only known at PPN sites in Lebanon and Israel, where the skulls of ancestors were preserved for remembrance and worship. One skull with drill holes and cuts was strung up on a pillar. Decapitated heads are symbolised on Pillar 43 (*see page 16*), and on a broken T-pillar top found in Enclosure D.

A stone slab inscribed with a crude image of a 'birthing goddess' is one of the few female figures that has been found, along with a small goddess statue holding a human head (*see opposite*). The statue of a man with phallus is more representative of the fertility motifs across Taş Tepeler, perhaps echoing male dominance within a hunting culture (*see opposite*). It was not until Çatalhöyük, 2000 years later, that goddess worship became a defining cultural practice in the region.

Giant stone troughs found at Göbekli Tepe show traces of calcium oxalate, produced during the fermenting of grain. Processing large amounts of grain can produce ergot, a psychedelic mould which Albert Hoffman synthesised in the 20th century to make LSD. Were the Taş Tepeler ancients producing psychedelic beer? Could this explain the abstract imagery and unusual cultic practices? In Raqefet Cave in Israel, a 13,000-year-old beer residue (infused with ergot) was found and its use linked with a 'death cult.'

ABOVE: Artist's impression of ritual objects found across Göbekli Tepe. LEFT: The damaged stone 'Totem Pole' depicts, from top to bottom, a lion, leopard / bear (possibly holding a head), part of a human figure with arms holding the navel, below it another human holding a head or phallus, or giving birth. BELOW LEFT: In 2008, fragments of a stone plate, a grinding stone with ochre on it and a boar statue were found below one of the central T-pillars of Enclosure C.

LANGUAGE & SYMBOLS
the first pictographs & the name of god

An emerging hypothesis is that written language itself may have originated at Göbekli Tepe. Numerous symbols and inscriptions, as observed by JJ Ainsworth and others, resemble Anatolian hieroglyphs ('Luwian') which first appear some 8000 years after Göbekli Tepe.

Dr. Manu Seyfzadeh and Prof. Robert Schoch suggest that symbols on Pillar 18 and Pillar 28 translate as "god" and "god of gods"—the oldest known mention of 'god'. Other pictographs could be early forms of written communication or numbering systems (*see opposite*).

Klaus Schmidt and science writer Lynne Kelly believe Göbekli Tepe was a monumental memory space, used for information transfer in non-literate societies. It holds records of animals, hunting, plants, landscape, cosmology, cataclysms and ancestral history. Later Taş Tepeler populations replicated the same memory systems in their own settlements and monuments. Burying the sites was a way to preserve this carefully collected knowledge for future generations.

Göbekli Tepe could be the apex of a relatively short-lived highculture, or the continuation of a more ancient Paleolithic lineage.

Some imagery from Taş Tepeler recurs at later sites in the region, and as far away as the Indus Valley (*see below*).

LEFT: Circle with dot and crescent beneath an 'H' on Pillar 18. Schoch believes it states that the god in question rules the cosmos, meaning "god of gods."
RIGHT: The top symbol, a Luwian Hieroglyph can be translated to "god" (2 crescents and 2 vertical lines). On Pillar 28 (page 56) similar symbols are carved vertically.
BELOW: The 'belt' of Pillar 18 includes an 'H' with a crescent either side, possibly denoting God.

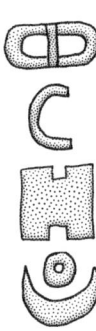

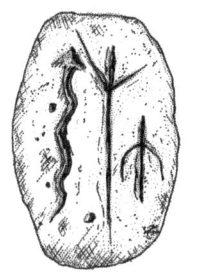

FAR LEFT: Plaquette with depiction of a snake, human and bird carved on a schist-type stone, all symbols related to the Scorpius constellation. LEFT: Serpents and chevrons on a another plaquette. Both from Göbekli Tepe.

FACING PAGE L to R: T-headed depictions from Mount Latmos, Turkey, c.6000 BC; Lengyel Vase inscription c.5000 BC; Indus Valley Plaquettes c.3200 BC, with T-headed figures, the left example is flanked by two scorpions. (see Pillar 43, p.17); The God Ea (Enki) with a T-shaped head from Khorsabad, late 8th century BC, Iraq.

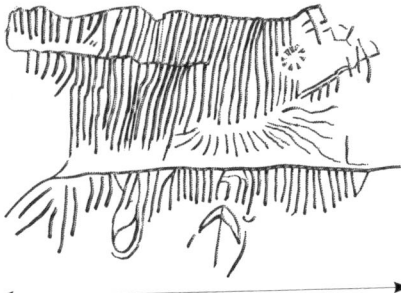

6 feet (1.8m)

LEFT: Lines and symbols carved into the bedrock at the peak of Karahan Tepe, with serpent head at its base. Early language, a counting device or a calendar recording lunar cycles?

WHO WERE THE BUILDERS?
migration & innovation

Who built Göbekli Tepe? Did nearby societies migrate there? Or was it constructed by people native to the Taş Tepeler region?

The Natufian culture (c.13,000 – 9500 BC) supported a sedentary population before the transition to agriculture; they occupied sites such as Tell Abu Hureyra in Syria, 70 miles (113 km) from Göbekli Tepe. Nothing they built approaches the scale of Göbekli Tepe, but they may have been ancestors of this later culture. Genetic studies show that 90% of Anatolian farmers are related to Natufian hunter-gatherers; 10% are from a gene pool in Iran and the Caucasus.

Andrew Collins contends that a lineage can be traced to ancient Northern European tribal migrations (*see map opposite*). Prof. Semih Güneri of Dokuz Eylül University analysed microblade stone tools which originated in Siberia 30,000 years ago. Over 15,000 years this 'technology' spread westward to the Zagros Mountains, eventually meeting the hunter-gatherers of southeastern Anatolia. Schmidt and Collins note that Helwan points (a type of early arrowhead found in Egypt), were discovered at Yenimahalle in Şanlıurfa c.8700 BC, suggesting a later Egyptian adoption.

 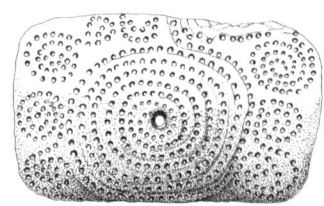

ANCIENT GEODESY
alignments & global connections

How far did the Taş Tepeler culture extend? Intriguingly, similar or identical art and symbology are found at other ancient sites around the globe. Easter Island's Moai statues have the same long-fingered hands touching the belly as found at Göbekli Tepe (*e, opposite*), and statues on Sulawesi in Indonesia have similar relief carvings (*i*). Carvings at Cutimbo, Sillustani and the Coricancha in Peru also have a remarkably similar style to Göbekli Tepe (*c.*). Symbols on Pillar 28 in Enclosure C matches a Worgaia Aborigine elder's body paint (*j.*). The 'bags' on Pillar 43 may be early depictions of the Sumerian 'bags' carried by the Anunnaki deities (*k.*).

Geodetic distances also appear. The surface distance from Göbekli Tepe to the Coricancha in Cusco, Peru (also meaning 'navel/centre') is equal to the equatorial diameter of the Earth, 7928 miles (12,759 km). Other examples are shown opposite in various ancient measures.

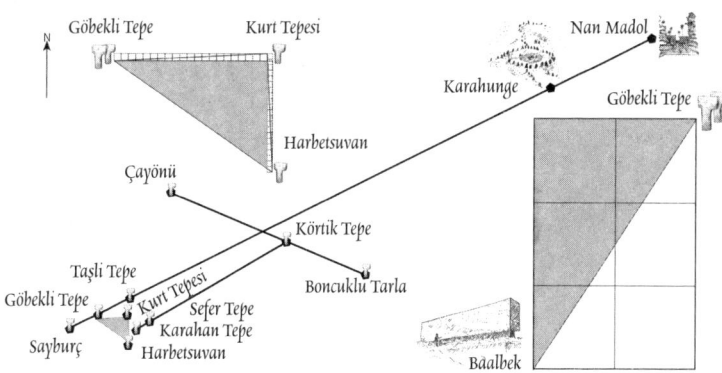

 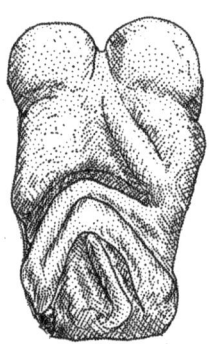

ABOVE LEFT: Enki with the Tigris and Euphrates rivers flowing into each of his shoulders. ABOVE RIGHT: Natufian 'lovers' sculpture from Ain Sakhri in Israel, 10cm (4in) tall, c. 9000 BC. They built circular stone houses and ritually buried their dead.

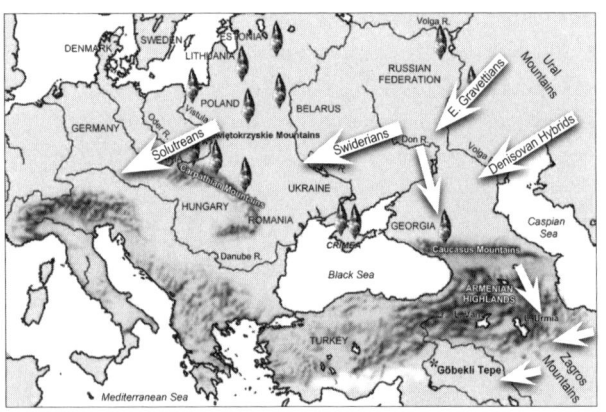

ABOVE: Migrations linked with microblade tools. RIGHT: The 2.8m (9.2ft) long wooden 'Shigir Idol', an 11,500 year old sculpture found in a peat bog in the Southern Ural Mountains. Similar to Taş Tepeler totem poles, with hands on the navel. FACING PAGE: Ivory plaque from Siberian settlement of Mal'ta, c.22,000 BC, with serpent symbolism and cup-marks.

THE EXPANSION
& *the megalithic explosion*

After carefully burying sites like Göbekli Tepe, their inhabitants seem to have moved elsewhere. To the west, Aşıklı Höyük (c.8000 BC) and Çatalhöyük (c.7500 BC) developed into sophisticated towns, incorporating many elements from the Taş Tepeler settlements. The huge underground city of Derinkuyu in Cappadocia uses techniques first seen at Karahan Tepe.

Throughout the Bible Lands, key sites such as Jericho (c.8300 BC), Atlit Yam (a submerged stone circle, c.7000 BC), and Karahunge in Armenia (c.6000 BC) all come after Göbekli Tepe. Migrations and knowledge transfer may have extended to the Caucasus, Iran, Central Asia, the Mediterranean coasts, even western Europe—10,000-year-old post holes have been found at Stonehenge (*roofed below, after Sarah Ewbank*).

Thriving at the end of the last Ice Age, Göbekli Tepe's innovative builders left a remarkable legacy.

Their long forgotten endeavours are now rewriting history.

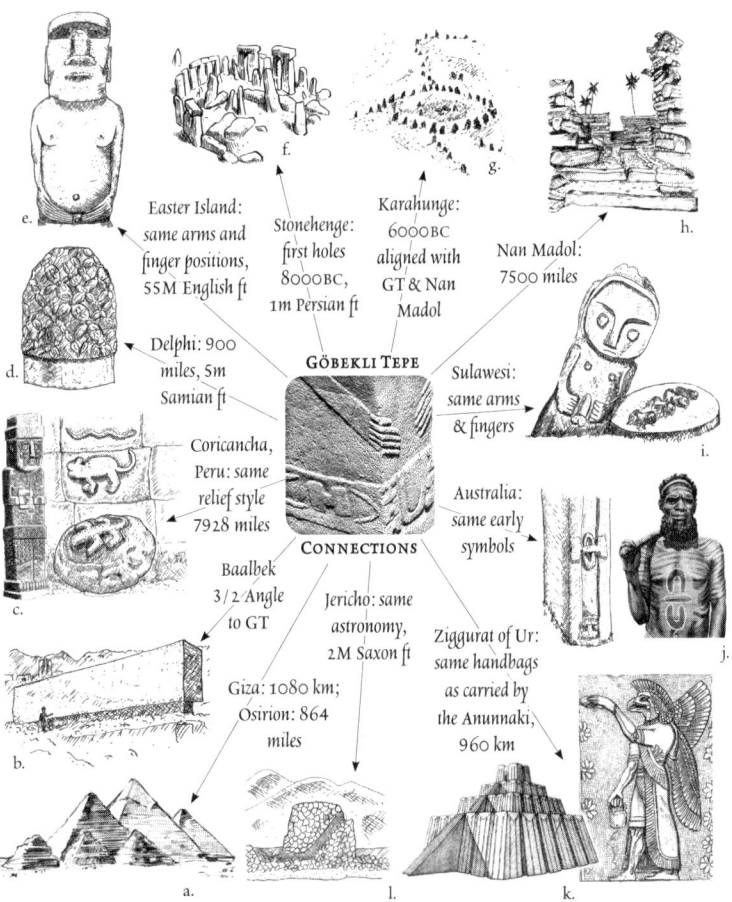

ABOVE: Geodetic plan of how Göbekli Tepe relates to other sites worldwide. FACING PAGE: Long distance alignments. One links Sayburç–Göbekli Tepe–Taşlı Tepe–Lake Van–Karahunge, Armenia–Nan Madol, Micronesia (7500 miles away). Howard Crowhurst has shown how a 2:3 triangle (shaded) connects Göbekli Tepe, Kurt Tepesi and Harbetsuvan, and also Baalbek in Lebanon to Göbekli Tepe.